Taking Off

Carmel Reilly
Karen Young

Rigby

www.Rigby.com
1-800-531-5015

Rigby Focus Forward

This Edition © 2009 Rigby, a Harcourt Education Imprint

Published in 2007 by Nelson Australia Pty Ltd ACN: 058 280 149
A Cengage Learning company

All rights reserved. No part of the material protected by this copyright may be
reproduced or utilized in any form or by any means, in whole or in part, without
permission in writing from the copyright owner. Requests for permission should be
mailed to: Paralegal Department, 6277 Sea Harbor Drive, Orlando, FL 32887.

Rigby is a trademark of Harcourt, registered in the United States of America and/or
other jurisdictions.

1 2 3 4 5 6 7 8 374 14 13 12 11 10 09 08 07
Printed and bound in China

Taking Off
ISBN-13   978-1-4190-3690-3
ISBN-10   1-4190-3690-4

If you have received these materials as examination copies free of charge, Rigby
retains title to the materials and they may not be resold. Resale of examination
copies is strictly prohibited and is illegal.

Possession of this publication in print format does not entitle users to convert this
publication, or any portion of it, into electronic format.

Carmel Reilly
Karen Young

Contents

Chapter 1 **The New Skateboard** 4

Chapter 2 **Come Back!** 8

Chapter 3 **Getting the Money** 12

The New Skateboard

Anna jumped on her new skateboard and raced down the hill.

"Hey!" she shouted to some kids who were out on the street. They all turned around as Anna came up to them.

The New Skateboard

"Cool skateboard," said her friend Mick as she stopped.

"Thanks," said Anna.
"I just got it."

Taking Off

Anna picked up her skateboard
and passed it to Mick.
He looked at it and passed it around.

Tom was the last kid to look at it.
He said, "Can I take it for a ride?"

"No," said Anna.
"It's a really, really cool skateboard,
and I don't want anything
to happen to it."

"I'm not going to let anything
happen to it," said Tom.
He dropped the skateboard
and put his foot on top of it.

The New Skateboard

Chapter 2

Come Back!

Tom really wanted to take a ride.

"Hey," said Anna. "I said 'no'!"

"Oh, come on …" said Tom,
and he raced off down the street.

Come Back!

"Come back!" shouted Anna.
"You don't even have a helmet!"

"Here," said Mick, passing Anna
his skateboard.

She grabbed it and raced off after Tom.

Taking Off

Anna could see Tom up ahead.

"Hey! Look out for the bump!" she shouted.

Tom looked back.
He was shocked to see Anna behind him.

"Look out!" Anna shouted again.

But it was too late.
Tom went over the bump and fell off.

Getting the Money

Tom was sitting on the ground.
"Are you okay?" said Anna, running up to him.

Tom nodded.

Getting the Money

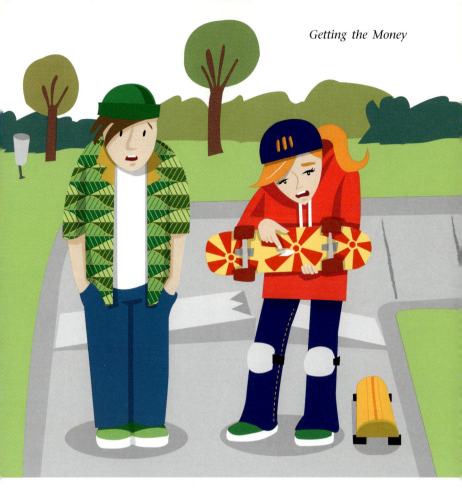

Anna looked at her skateboard,
as Tom was getting up.
A little bit of paint had come off it.

"Why did you take my skateboard?"
said Anna.

Taking Off

"I'm sorry.
I just wanted to take a ride.
My mom doesn't have the money
to get me a skateboard," said Tom.

"But you can't take people's things,"
said Anna.

"I'm really, really sorry," Tom said.

Getting the Money

"Not all of the money for my skateboard came from Mom and Dad," said Anna. "Most of it came from little jobs I did for people."

"Really?" said Tom.

"Yes, really," said Anna.

Tom looked at Anna.
"Hey, I could do some jobs
to get money, too," he said at last.

"Yes, you could," said Anna.
Then she smiled.
"And when you get your skateboard,
you can come ride with me."

Tom looked shocked,
then he smiled back.
"That would be really good," he said.
"I'd like that a lot."